7/15

It's My State!

RHODE ISLAND

The Ocean State

WITHDRAWN

Rick Petreycik, Lisa M. Herrington, and Hex Kleinmartin

Cavendish
Square

New York

Published in 2015 by Cavendish Square Publishing, LLC
243 5th Avenue, Suite 136, New York, NY 10016

Website: cavendishsq.com

This publication represents the opinions and views of the author based on his or her personal experience, knowledge, and research. The information in this book serves as a general guide only. The author and publisher have used their best efforts in preparing this book and disclaim liability rising directly or indirectly from the use and application of this book.

CPSIA Compliance Information: Batch #WW15CSQ

All websites were available and accurate when this book was sent to press.

Library of Congress Cataloging-in-Publication Data

Kleinmartin, Hex.
Rhode Island / Hex Kleinmartin, Rick Petreycik, Lisa M Herrington. — Third edition.
pages cm. — (It's my state!)
Petreycik's name appears first on earlier edition.
Includes bibliographical references and index.
ISBN 978-1-50260-024-0 (hardcover) ISBN 978-1-50260-025-7 (ebook)
1. Rhode Island—Juvenile literature. I. Petreycik, Rick. II. Herrington, Lisa M. III. Title.

F79.3.P48 2015
974.5—dc23

2014022992

Editor: Fletcher Doyle
Senior Copy Editor: Wendy A. Reynolds
Art Director: Jeffrey Talbot
Designer: Joseph Macri
Senior Production Manager: Jennifer Ryder-Talbot
Production Editor: David McNamara
Photo Research by J8 Media

The photographs in this book are used by permission and through the courtesy of: Cover photo by Aimin Tang/E+/Getty Images; Michael Westhoff/E+/Getty Images, 4; Superstock: Dennis Fast VWPics, 4 (top); Animal Animals, 4 (bottom); Alex Huck/ File:Cumberlandite. jpg/Wikimedia Commons, 5; Animal Animals, 5 (bottom); The Image Works: The National History Museum, 5 (top); Leightonoc/Shutterstock. com, 6; age fotostock, 8; Raymond Forbes/age fotostock, 9; Alamy: Alvis Upitis, 11; Travel Library Limited, 12; Ken Babbitt/Four Seam Images vs AP Images, 14; Lana Sundman, 14; Visions of America, 14; Infrogmation/File:Providence20June07ProvidenceTheaterB.jpg/Wikimedia Commons, 15; WFProvidence/File:Waterfire flicker image 4.jpg/Wikimedia Commons, 15; Peter Casolino 15 (center); Image Source, 16; VC Ross/Prisma, 17; Peter Hvizdak, 18; Minden Pictures 19; iStockphoto.com/Paolo2710, 20; Juniors Bildarchiv, 20; Animal Animals, 20 (center); Graceson/Shutterstock.com, 21; John Gerlach/Visuals Unlimited/Getty Images, 21; Robert McGouey/All Canada Photos, 21 (top); North Wind Picture Archives, 22; James Lemass, 24; North Wind Picture Archives, 25; North Wind Picture Archives, 26; North Wind Picture Archives, 28; North Wind Picture Archives, 29; Epitavi/iStock/Thinkstock, 30; Superstock, 32; North Wind Picture Archives, 33; Sean Pavone/Shutterstock. com, 34; Anthony Ricci/Shutterstockcom, 34; Swampyank/File:Governor William Sprague Mansion House at 1351 Cranston Street Cranston, Rhode Island RI USA.jpg/Wikimedia Commons, 34; Marcbela/File:Downtown Woonsocket Historic District.jpg/Wikimedia Commons, 35; Amanda Cournoyer/File:GeneralNathanaelGreeneHomestead.jpg/Wikimedia Commons, 35; Marc N. Belanger/File:Cumberland Town Hall RI.jpg/WIkimedia Commons, 35; Stock Montage/Archive Photos/Getty Images, 37; DigitalVues, 38; Everett Collection, 39; Everett Collection Inc, 40; J. Rowan/Photri Images, 42; Stephen Simpson, 44; File:Kady Brownell CDV.jpg/Wikimedia Commons, 48; Carl Van Vechten/Library of Congress, 48; Everett Collection Inc, 48; Everett Collection, 48 (bottom); Frazer Harrison/Getty Images, 49; Getty Images: Getty Images, 49 (top); National Photo Gallery, 49; age fotostock, 50; John Phelan/File:St. Ann's Church, Woodsocket RI.jpg/Wikimedia Commons, 51; Christian Science Monitor, 52; Courtesy of Mary-Beth DeGrange, 54; Courtesy of MouseWorks Photography, 55; David Wells, 55; CQ-Roll Call Group, 56; age fotostock, 58; age fotostock, 59; Associated Press, 61; File:Lincoln Chafee official portrait.jpg/Wikimedia Commons, 62; State of Rhode Island, 62; Associated Press, 62; Courtesy Mary Beth Meehan/UPP Arts, 63; Corbis: Marianne Lee/AgStock Images, 64; Raymond Forbes/age fotostock, 67; William K. Derby/America 24-7/Getty Images, 68; MCT/McClatchy-Tribune/Getty Images, 68; Bob Rowan, Progressive Images, 69 (top); Associated Press, 69 (center); mama_mia/Shutterstock.com, 70; Bob Rowan, Progressive Images, 71; Visions of America, 72; Associated Press, 73; mcdonojj/ Shutterstock.com, 75; Kenneth C. Zirkel/iStock/Thinkstock, 75.

Printed in the United States of America

RHODE ISLAND
CONTENTS

★ State Tree: Red Maple

The red maple, widespread in Rhode Island, was officially made the state tree in 1964. In the fall, its leaves turn brilliant colors of gold, purple, and red.

★ State Flower: Violet

Rhode Island was the last state to adopt an official state flower. Although schoolchildren chose the violet as the state flower in 1897, it did not officially become the state flower until 1968. Violets have striking deep purple or blue petals.

★ State Bird: Rhode Island Red

Rhode Island's state bird is actually a special breed of chicken introduced on a farm in Little Compton in the 1850s. Known for its tasty meat and eggs, it was chosen as the state bird in 1954.

RHODE ISLAND
POPULATION: 1,052,567

★ State Mineral: Bowenite

Bowenite is named after George Bowen, a Rhode Island geologist who discovered the mineral in the early 1800s. Similar to jade, bowenite is found mainly in northern sections of Rhode Island. This mineral typically ranges in color from green to yellow.

★ State Rock: Cumberlandite

Scientists estimate that cumberlandite rocks, used to make cannonballs during the American Revolution, are a little more than one billion years old. The rocks are usually dark brown or black with white and gray markings. Cumberlandite became the state's official rock in 1966.

★ State Shell: Quahog

The quahog is a thick-shelled, edible clam found along Narragansett Bay. In 1987, Rhode Island named the quahog its official state shell. **Native Americans** used quahog shells to make wampum beads, which served as money.

Population Data: U.S. Bureau of the Census, 2010

A Quick Look at Rhode Island 5

Ocean racing has a long and glorious history in Rhode Island.

The
Ocean State

No matter where you are in Rhode Island, you are never far from the water. It is easy to see why Rhode Island has been nicknamed the Ocean State. Rhode Island is the smallest of the fifty states. It is only 48 miles (77 kilometers) from north to south and 37 miles (60 km) from east to west, and is home to just over one million people (1,052,567 in 2010).

A person can drive across the entire state in less than an hour. The state is divided into five counties. Rhode Island's land area spans 1,034 square miles (2,678 square kilometers). About 425 Rhode Islands could fit inside the largest U.S. state, Alaska. Because of its small size, the state is also called "Little Rhody."

Size is not what defines Rhode Island, however. Rhode Island has played a big role in American history. It is the birthplace of religious freedom in what is now the United States. In 1776, Rhode Island was the first of the original thirteen colonies to declare independence from Great Britain.

America's factory system also traces its roots to Rhode Island. The country's first water-powered cotton mill was built here in the late eighteenth century. A mill is a factory that processes a raw material, such as cotton, paper, or steel. The Rhode Island mill introduced the United States to the **Industrial Revolution**. During this era, **manufacturing** shifted from making goods using hand tools in homes or small shops to large-scale production in factories.

Castle Hill Lighthouse on Narragansett Bay was opened in 1890.

Rhode Island Borders

North:	Massachusetts
South:	Atlantic Ocean
East:	Massachusetts
West:	Connecticut

Just as interesting as Rhode Island's rich history is its impressive geography. Sounds, bays, inlets, and the Atlantic Ocean border Rhode Island. The jagged shores along Narragansett Bay and the state's thirty-plus islands form a **coastline** of more than 400 miles (640 km).

Rhode Island is one of six states that make up the northeastern region of the United States known as New England. The others are Connecticut, Maine, Massachusetts, New Hampshire, and Vermont. From its historic landmarks to its scenic shores, the Ocean State is filled with many exciting attractions for residents and visitors alike.

Shaping the State

Most of Rhode Island's natural features are a result of the movement of **glaciers**, which are rivers of ice. Thousands of years ago, huge glaciers slowly expanded their reach south from Canada and covered much of the northeastern United States. As they moved, the glaciers cut into the solid rock that lay beneath loose surface material. They also helped shape hills, carrying sand, clay, and rocks.

As the glaciers began to melt and retreat back toward the north, the melting ice formed rivers that washed gravel, sand, and other material onto the surrounding plains. It pushed up rocky cliffs and carved out lakes and ponds. The rushing water also created channels leading to the ocean. Natural changes to the land are responsible for many of Rhode Island's inland bodies of water. However, some of the state's water bodies are human-made lakes, or reservoirs. Altogether, there are more than three hundred reservoirs, ponds, and natural freshwater lakes in Rhode Island. The movement of glaciers formed Rhode Island's two land regions. They are the Coastal Lowlands and the Eastern New England Upland.

Providence is Rhode Island's capital and commercial center.

RHODE ISLAND
COUNTY MAP

PROVIDENCE

BRISTOL

KENT

NEWPORT

WASHINGTON

WASHINGTON

RHODE ISLAND
POPULATION BY COUNTY

Bristol County	49,875	Providence County	626,667
Kent County	166,158	Washington County	126,979
Newport County	82,888		

Source: U.S. Bureau of the Census, 2010

Narragansett Bay is New England's largest estuary at 147 square miles (380 sq. km).

Newport, which is located on Aquidneck Island, was founded in 1639.

The Coastal Lowlands

The flat Coastal Lowlands cover much of Rhode Island. Most of the state's major cities and tourist attractions are located in this area. The lowlands include the eastern section of the state and all of its islands. The Coastal Lowlands region is made up mostly of sandy beaches, saltwater ponds, marshes, and lagoons. The state's lowest point is at sea level in the lowlands.

Narragansett Bay is a stretch of water that extends north from the Atlantic Ocean and practically cuts the state in two. Narragansett Bay is connected to other smaller bays, such as Greenwich Bay and Mount Hope Bay, and many rivers, including the Providence River. East of the bay, the hills are rounded and wooded. To the west of the bay, the area has denser forests. Farther west, the ground gradually increases in elevation.

Providence is Rhode Island's capital, and is located on the mainland near the Providence River. Other towns and cities on the mainland in the coastal lowlands include Warwick, Cranston, Woonsocket, Charlestown, and Westerly.

In and around Narragansett Bay are several islands. Some of these islands are home to towns and cities. Aquidneck Island, the largest island, includes Newport, Portsmouth, and Middletown. Newport is one of Rhode Island's most famous cities. A popular tourist destination, Newport has played a big role in the state's history.

All of the state's islands are located in, or border, Narragansett Bay except for Block Island. This popular vacation spot is the state's southernmost point. It is located in the Atlantic Ocean, about 12 miles (19 km) from the Rhode Island coast and is only 7 miles (11 km) long and 3 miles (5 km) wide. It is not connected to the mainland by any bridges or tunnels. The only way to get there is by plane or boat. Ferries carry visitors to Block Island. Nature trails, historic buildings, lighthouses, and other tourist attractions are found on the island. It is also home to about eight hundred year-round residents who have their own town government, school system, and other public services.

The Eastern New England Upland

The Eastern New England Upland, which extends from Connecticut to Maine, stretches through the northern and western regions of Rhode Island. It covers about one-third of the state's total area. Rolling hills, narrow valleys, wooded areas, ponds, lakes, and reservoirs mark this scenic region, which is also called the Western Rocky Upland. The area has higher elevations than the Coastal Lowlands. At 812 feet (247 m) above sea level, Jerimoth Hill is the highest point in Rhode Island.

Newport Beach provides relief from the heat on a summer day.

10 KEY SITES ★ ★ ★

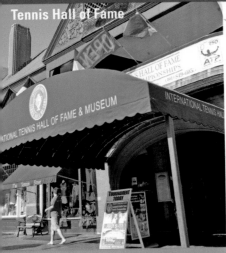
Tennis Hall of Fame

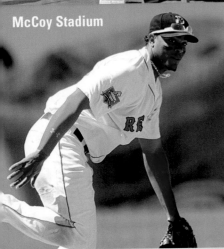
McCoy Stadium

The Breakers

1. Crescent Park Carousel

Little kids love riding on carousels, and Rhode Island has some great ones. The Crescent Park Carousel in East Providence was built in 1895 by famous carousel designer Charles I. D. Loof and has been lovingly maintained over the years.

2. International Tennis Hall of Fame

The museum has a large collection of tennis memorabilia, including a fun exhibit of tennis fashions through the years. The beautiful grounds in Newport include thirteen grass tennis courts that host a major professional tournament.

3. McCoy Stadium

More than 500,000 people head to McCoy Stadium each year to watch the Pawtucket Red Sox, the farm club for the Boston Red Sox. Baseball's "Longest Game" was played here in 1981. Lasting a record thirty-three innings, it took more than eight hours over two days to complete.

4. The Museum of Natural History and Planetarium

This Providence museum is the only one in Rhode Island dedicated to natural history and is home to the state's only public planetarium. The collections include fossils, minerals, rocks, and other artifacts. A Zeiss star projector projects the stars on the Planetarium's domed ceiling.

5. Newport Mansions

The Newport **Mansions** are among the state's best-known attractions. The Preservation Society of Newport County operates nine homes that were once the "summer cottages" of America's wealthiest families, including The Breakers, Marble House, The Elms, and Rosecliff.

6. Providence Children's Museum

The Providence Children's Museum is one of the best Rhode Island attractions for children. You can have fun playing in the water area, crawling though subterranean tunnels, and climbing the new one-of-a-kind play sculpture.

7. Providence Performing Arts Center

The performing arts are a big draw in Providence. People flock to the Providence Performing Arts Center to see Broadway shows, concerts, plays, and more. These include classical music performances by the Rhode Island Philharmonic and others.

8. Rhode Island Beaches

The state has 400 miles of coastline and more than one hundred salt and freshwater beaches. The Third Beach in Middletown is a good family beach, while the Mohegan Bluffs Beach on Block Island is a more hidden, quiet beach.

9. Roger Williams Park Zoo

The Roger Williams Park Zoo, which opened in 1872 in Providence, is one of our nation's oldest zoos and has been named the "finest zoo in New England" by *The Boston Globe*. It contains more than one hundred species of animals.

10. WaterFire in Providence

Seen on select evenings (usually between May and October) WaterFire is a seasonal, multi-sensory art installation where volunteer "firetenders" travel on torch-lit boats, lighting more than eighty bonfires as mystical music fills the air.

Providence Performing Arts Center

Mohegan Bluffs Beach

WaterFire

A part of the Pawtuxet River was dammed to create the Scituate Reservoir.

The western portion of the state is dotted with small towns and cities, rivers, reservoirs, and lakes. Much of the land is ideal for growing hay, corn, and potatoes. The wooded areas in the region are filled with a variety of trees, including oak, maple, hickory, birch, pine, spruce, cedar, and hemlock. Parts of Rhode Island's Upland are perfect for those who enjoy outdoor activities such as hiking, canoeing, fishing, and horseback riding.

Climate

Rhode Island's **climate** tends to be milder than that of its New England neighbors. This means that Rhode Island usually has warmer winter temperatures. The higher temperatures are a result of the winds blowing in from the Atlantic Ocean and Narragansett Bay. The northern and northwestern sections of Rhode Island tend to have cooler year-round temperatures than southern and coastal Rhode Island. In the summer, the coast and the southern portions of the state are slightly warmer than the northern sections.

In general, the coldest months in the state are January and February. During January, Rhode Islanders can expect an average temperature of about 29° Fahrenheit (–2° Celsius). The lowest temperature in the state occurred on February 5, 1996, when the city of Greene recorded a frigid –25°F (–32°C).

The warmest months in Rhode Island are July and August. The average July temperature is 73°F (23°C). The heat became pretty intense for residents of Providence on August 2, 1975, when the temperature climbed to a record-breaking 104°F (40°C).

Precipitation is the amount of water that falls as rain, snow, or other moisture. Rhode Island's average precipitation is about 47 inches (119 centimeters) per year, though the southwestern part tends to be wetter than the rest of the state. Annual snowfall in the state amounts to about 31 inches (79 cm).

Hurricanes and floods have been the fiercest weather events that Rhode Islanders living in coastal areas have had to deal with over the years. Hurricanes usually strike in late summer and early fall. Strong hurricane winds can damage or destroy homes and other buildings. The heavy rains and strong, tall waves from hurricanes often cause flooding and structural damage to buildings. Throughout Rhode Island's history, hurricanes have caused millions of dollars of damage.

Wildflowers add color to Rhode Island's fields and forests.

Harbor seals lounge on the rocks on Block Island.

Wildlife

Rhode Island hosts a wide variety of plants and animals. More than 60 percent of the state is forested. Around sixty different species, or types, of trees thrive in Rhode Island. They include ashes, hickories, elms, maples, poplars, beeches, willows, birches, and Atlantic white cedars. In the warm-weather months, inland fields are often dotted with colorful wildflowers, such as goldenrod, asters, violets, and lilies. Flowering plants also populate the state's wooded areas. Among these are mountain laurels, wild roses, dogwoods, azaleas, blue gentians, orchids, irises, and rhododendrons.

Many wild mammals roam Rhode Island's wooded areas as well. They include white-tailed deer, skunks, rabbits, raccoons, squirrels, moles, foxes, and woodchucks. Beavers, muskrats, otters, and mink can be spotted swimming in the state's ponds, rivers, and lakes. Other inhabitants of these freshwater areas include fish such as bass, perch, pike, trout, and pickerel.

The salty coastal waters are home to swordfish, striped bass, flounder, shark, tuna, mackerel, jellyfish, bluefish, cod, and butterfish. Shellfish also thrive, particularly lobsters, soft-shell crabs, oysters, scallops, mussels, and clams. During winter months, harbor seals can be found lounging on Block Island's rocks and beaches.

More than four hundred species of birds have been spotted in the state. Inhabiting Rhode Island's wooded areas are robins, owls, blue jays, flickers, sparrows, and catbirds. Looking for meals of fish and shellfish along the coast are seagulls, terns, osprey, and loons. Geese and ducks live near the state's waterways. Rhode Island also has some game birds, including pheasants, quails, and partridges, that are hunted during specific times of the year.

Wildlife at Risk

Rhode Island has gone to great lengths to protect its wildlife. However, increasing pollution has put some types of wildlife in the state in danger of disappearing completely from their ranges. When a type of animal or plant is endangered, it is at risk of dying out in its range or a large area of its range. A threatened species is at risk of becoming endangered. Rhode Island has several endangered species, including the roseate tern, the American burying beetle, and three types of sea turtles.

The American burying beetle, which lives on Block Island, is among Rhode Island's endangered species.

10 KEY PLANTS AND ANIMALS

Bluefish

Blue Jay

Eastern Purple Bladderwort

1. Bluefish

Bluefish are a common sight along Rhode Island's Atlantic coastline, particularly in the spring when they prey on other fish moving toward the shore to breed. Fishing for bluefish and their young, known as snappers, is a popular sport in Rhode Island.

2. Blue Jay

People recognize this woodland bird, which is part of the crow family, by its bright blue, black, and white color and the pointy crest at the top of its head. Blue jays may be as long as 12 inches (30 cm).

3. Chairmaker's Bulrush

Chairmaker's bulrush is a species of flowering plant in the sedge family. Native American groups used this plant for food, basketry, and hat making, and chair makers from colonial times to the present use it for woven cane chair seats.

4. Eastern Purple Bladderwort

This medium-sized suspended aquatic carnivorous plant lives in water and not only produces its own food from sunlight, but also can use its bladders to digest insects. It tends to catch very few insects compared to other carnivorous plants.

5. Goldenrod

Goldenrod is a wildflower that graces Rhode Island's meadows, woods, and hills in autumn. It has a wand-like stem with clusters of brilliant yellow flowers. The plant can grow to a height of 4 feet (1.2 m).

6. Muskrat

This large rodent, covered with brownish fur, can grow to more than 14 inches (36 cm) long. Muskrats make their homes around Rhode Island's numerous ponds, lakes, and rivers by piecing together piles of twigs, branches, leaves, and other plant material.

7. North American River Otter

This otter is protected and insulated by a thick, water-repellent coat of fur. Equally at home in the water and on land, otters establish burrows close to the water's edge in rivers, lakes, swamps, coastal shorelines, tidal flats, or estuary ecosystems.

8. Paper Birch

Sometimes called white birches or canoe birches, paper birch trees have sheets of bark that peel off in layers and remind people of sheets of paper. In the past, Native Americans used the sturdy but flexible bark of these tall trees to build canoes.

9. Rhode Island Red

The Rhode Island Red is a utility bird, raised for meat and eggs. By 1903, this solid breed of chicken was known for its deep color, strong constitution, and relatively hard feathers, and prized by farmers for laying lots of brown eggs.

10. White-Tailed Deer

These graceful, swift animals have red-brown fur in the summer that changes to a grayish brown during the winter. An adult male deer, or buck, can weigh nearly 300 pounds (140 kilograms).

Muskrat

North American River Otter

Paper Birch

Roger Williams fled Massachusetts and established good relations with the Narragansett.

From the Beginning

Many historians and scientists estimate that the first humans arrived in the region that now includes Rhode Island around 8,000 BCE. These people were the ancestors of present-day Native Americans. They were mainly hunters and gatherers who looked for food in the area's thick forests and coastal waters. They lived in small communities and made tools out of stone and grew crops such as corn, beans, squash, cucumbers, tobacco, and pumpkins.

In the early seventeenth century, about ten thousand Native Americans lived in the area. They made up four main tribes: the Nipmuc, Niantic, Wampanoag, and Narragansett.

Except for occasional battles between the Narragansett (the largest and most powerful group in the region) and the Wampanoag (who inhabited the far eastern parts), the tribes lived peacefully.

The First European Settlers

The first known European to explore the area was an Italian sailing for France named Giovanni da Verrazzano, who in 1524, landed near Block Island. In 1614, Dutch sea captain Adriaen Block became the next European arrival. Block Island is named after him.

A statue of Rhode Island's founder stands in Roger Williams Park in Providence.

In 1630, about one thousand Puritans left England to start a colony in Massachusetts. A colony is land settled and governed by another country. The Puritans had left England because they disagreed with the Church of England. They believed in firm obedience to church laws, which were strictly enforced by their colony's governor, John Winthrop.

Rhode Island's Founder: Roger Williams

In 1631, Roger Williams, an English preacher, arrived in Boston. He believed in religious freedom—that individuals should be free to worship God however they desire, and that the laws of a church and of government should be separate. In addition, Williams, who had made friends with Native Americans and respected their way of life, thought white **settlers** should treat them fairly and pay them for land taken by settlers.

Williams's beliefs conflicted with those of the Puritan leaders of the Massachusetts Bay Colony. Officials arrested him on several occasions, finally banishing him in 1635. Before Williams could be sent back to England, he fled south. In a few days, he arrived at the eastern side of Narragansett Bay, where the Wampanoag and their leader, Massasoit, welcomed him. He also met the Narragansetts.

Other white settlers seeking religious freedom soon joined Williams. In June 1636, he purchased land from Massasoit and two Narragansett leaders, Canonicus and Miantonomo. Thus, Williams created the first permanent settlement in Rhode Island. He named it Providence, as he felt that God's "watchful eye" had kept him safe and guided him on his trip from Boston. Other settlements soon sprang up in the area that now includes Portsmouth, Newport, and Warwick.

Grim Reminder

The oldest known war monument to veterans in the United States is in Cumberland. A cairn of stones was erected in memory of the colonists killed in Pierce's Fight during King Philip's War in 1676. It is known as Nine Men's Misery monument for those tortured to death.

In 1634, Anne Hutchinson (1591–1643) moved with her family from England to the Massachusetts Bay Colony in search of religious freedom. She challenged the religious views of Puritan leaders with her preaching. Puritan officials believed that women should not be able to preach. Like Roger Williams, Hutchinson was banned from the colony.

Anne Hutchinson faced two trials before being banished from Massachusetts.

The Native People

Tribes that lived in Rhode Island included the Narragansett (throughout the state, but mostly to the west of Narragansett Bay all the way to Connecticut), the Eastern Niantic (along the southern coast), the Nipmuc (along the northern border of the state), and the Wampanoag (along the eastern boarder of the state). All of these groups were a part of the Algonquians, a large collection of northeastern tribes that shared customs and related languages.

They were a hunting and farming people by the time Europeans began to visit North America. Women harvested maize (hard corn), squash and beans and also gathered nuts and fruit, while men did most of the hunting. They shot deer, turkeys, and small game, and went fishing, with those on the coast often fishing from dugout canoes. Children often collected other food such as berries, nuts and herbs. In the coastal areas, people would build wigwams or *wetus*, which are 8 to 10 feet (2.4 to 3 m) tall with a domed roof. These were built from a wooden pole framework and covered with birch bark and woven mats, and would house a family. Farther inland, people also built **longhouses**, which had straight walls and curved roofs but could be 20 feet (6 m) wide and 20 feet (6 m) tall and up to 200 feet (61 m) long. While the small houses would be comfortable for a single family for several months, the longhouses could hold many families and be

Roger Williams lands at Providence in 1636.

permanent living spaces. Most of the Native Americans living in the region settled in villages near water, which gave them easy access to sources of food and trade. They also had a system of government in which village leaders who functioned as judges resolved legal and spiritual disputes.

The Native tribes were practically wiped out in King Philip's War. The Native Americans who remained did not have much power against the white settlers. Some moved away, while others gave up their lifestyles to fit in with the colonists.

The Narragansett is the only federally recognized Native American tribe left in the state.

The Narragansett

Narragansett is pronounced "nair-uh-GANN-set." It comes from the Narragansett place name naiaganset, which means "small point of land." The Narragansett were known as warriors, and offered protection to the Niantic.

Distribution: Currently, the Narragansett occupy the Narragansett Indian **Reservation**, 1,800 acres (7.3 sq. km) of trust lands in Charlestown, and have several hundred acres in Westerly. The group has just over two thousand members, and the main community is at Charlestown.

Homes: The Narragansett favored longhouses and wetus for their villages. Many families would live together for long periods of time.

Food: The Narragansett grew the "three sisters" of maize, squash, and beans, which were all planted together and helped each other grow. They also hunted deer, turkeys, squirrels, rabbits, and other small animals, as well as fished and gathered clams.

Clothing: Narragansett men wore breech-cloths, while women wore skirts to their knees, and all wore moccasins. Shirts were not usually worn, but in colder weather people wore deerskin capes. Women usually had long hair, but men, especially warriors, might shave all but one small area of their head and keep the remaining hair long to produce a *scalplock*.

Art: The Narragansett, like most coastal northeastern Native Americans, did beadwork and made wampum from shell beads that could be used for messages or as money. They also wove decorative beads.

With the help of Williams, she and her followers founded present-day Portsmouth in Rhode Island in 1638. (Other Hutchinson followers headed south and founded Newport in 1639.) After her husband's death, Hutchinson moved to Long Island in New York. She was killed in 1643 during a fight with Native Americans.

The Charters

In 1644, the English Parliament granted Williams a written assurance of rights called a charter. The charter recognized the four settlements of Providence, Portsmouth, Newport, and Warwick as the colony of Providence Plantations, which in 1647 officially united. Representatives from each settlement met at Portsmouth. They set up a system of government that included a representative assembly and a president, who would be elected by the male inhabitants.

By the 1650s, Roger Williams's vision of religious freedom and tolerance for all made Rhode Island a popular place for people of different faiths. In 1663, King Charles II of England granted the four settlements a new royal charter. The charter gave the colony the name *Rhode Island and Providence Plantations*. It provided the new colony with more self-government than any of the other colonies. The charter also authorized the colony to continue Roger Williams's "lively experiment" of freedom of religion for all.

Roger Williams returned from England in 1644 with a royal charter to establish the colony of Rhode Island.

A fight between settlers and Native Americans, known as King Philip's War, eventually spread to Rhode Island.

In Providence, in 1638, Williams established the first Baptist church in what is now the United States. Another group of Christians called Quakers built a meetinghouse on Aquidneck Island in 1657. People of the Jewish faith began settling in Rhode Island in the 1650s, and in 1763, the Touro Synagogue opened in Newport. It is the oldest Jewish house of worship in the United States, and is now a national historic site.

King Philip's War

For nearly forty years after Roger Williams founded Providence, Rhode Island's colonists had peaceful relations with the area's Native Americans. That is partly because Williams believed that, as the first inhabitants of the area, Native Americans were the rightful owners of the land and should be paid for losing it. However, settlers in other colonies started a war by taking land.

In 1675, Metacom, a Wampanoag leader whom the settlers called King Philip, began attacking English settlements. He convinced other groups in the region—the Nipmuc, Mohegan, and Podunk—to join him.

Making a Quill Pen

Many people in colonial Rhode Island wrote in their diary almost every day, and the instrument they used for writing was a quill pen. Here's how you can make one so you can write just as they did.

What You Need

Large goose, swan or turkey feathers (from a craft store)

Scissors or pen knife (ask an adult for help with the knife)

Tweezers

Washable ink

What You Do

- Turn the quill so its shaft curves downward. This will show you the bottom of the quill.

- Remove some of the feather from the bottom to make the pen easier to hold.

- Now, with the bottom facing up, cut the bottom of the quill at an acute, or sharp, angle from about an inch up the shaft to the tip.

- Use your tweezers to remove any material inside the quill.

- Cut approximately one-half inch (about 13 millimeters) off the front, forming a point.

- Cut a quarter-inch (about 6 mm) slit from the point straight up toward the feather. This will allow the ink to flow from the pen. Adjust by trimming the point to get a suitable writing point.

- Pour some washable ink into a container and test it out. You may find writing with the new pen a challenge, but keep at it!

At first, King Philip targeted only colonial settlements in Massachusetts Bay. That changed when militias from Connecticut and Massachusetts Bay attacked and defeated a group of warriors near a southern Rhode Island town now called Kingston. The battle became known as the Great Swamp Fight. The colonial militias did not stop there, continuing to raid and burn surrounding Native American villages. Within a few days, they had killed more than a thousand Native men, women, and children.

King Philip and his allies retaliated, attacking settlements and setting Providence on fire. Settlers from the town and neighboring areas were forced to flee to offshore islands. In 1676, King Philip was killed in a battle near present-day Bristol, Rhode Island. The series of battles between the Native American tribes and English colonists became known as King Philip's War.

The Narragansett, Wampanoag, Nipmuc, Mohegan, and Podunk groups were practically wiped out as a result of the war. Several hundred of King Philip's warriors were also captured and sold into slavery in other countries. The relationships between the Rhode Island colonists and the region's Native Americans were never the same.

The Triangle Trade

The early 1700s marked the beginning of a period of great prosperity for Rhode Island. The colony's **population** grew from just seven thousand people in 1710 to forty thousand in 1755. Farming and whaling were very profitable businesses. Candles and other products were made from whale oil. Through sea trading, the colony's merchants sold and traded everything from wood, salt, cider, dairy products, and molasses to horses, fish, and preserved meats. Rhode Island's coasts made it easy for ships to come in and sail out carrying a wide variety of goods. Within a short period of time, Newport and Providence emerged as bustling ports in colonial America.

Rhode Island merchants prospered from the slave trade. In fact, they controlled between 60 and 90 percent of the American trade in African slaves. Rhode Island's prosperity during this period depended on its trade relationship with the Caribbean West Indies called the Triangle Trade, whose three points were Rhode Island, Africa, and the Caribbean Islands.

Rhode Island merchants would send rum made in Rhode Island with molasses from the West Indies to Africa. Once the rum arrived in Africa, it was exchanged for African slaves. The slaves were shipped to the West Indies to work on the sugar plantations and traded for molasses. The molasses was then sent to Rhode Island and turned into rum.

Newport was one of the busiest ports in the colonies in the mid-1700s.

Slave ships were dirty and crowded. Many slaves died from the horrible conditions. Some slaves from Africa ended up working in Rhode Island. By 1774, slaves made up more than 6 percent of Rhode Island's population. In 1784, Rhode Island passed a law that freed the children of slaves. The international slave trade, however, continued into the 1800s.

Acts of Rebellion

Around that time, Great Britain was involved in a series of wars with France for control over much of North America. The last of these struggles was known as the French and Indian War (1754–1763). Great Britain defeated France, gaining almost all of France's land east of the Mississippi River. Great Britain expected its colonies to provide troops, and even after the fighting was over, Britain imposed fees and taxes on the colonists to help pay for the war.

In Their Own Words

"[Touro] is not only the oldest Synagogue in America but also one of the oldest symbols of liberty. No better tradition exists than the history of Touro Synagogue's great contribution to the goals of freedom and justice for all."

—John F. Kennedy, thirty-fifth president of the United States

Many colonists, however, opposed the new British taxes, feeling the war debt was Britain's responsibility. In 1764, the British Parliament passed the Sugar Act requiring the colonists to pay a tax on imported goods such as molasses, sugar, and wine. The next year, the British Parliament passed the Stamp Act, which taxed all paper items—from legal documents to playing cards—in the colonies. The colonists were angered even further.

In protest and to avoid paying taxes, some merchants smuggled molasses, sugar, and other taxable goods into the colony and the general unrest eventually led to violence. In 1769, colonists burned the British ship *Liberty* in Newport's waters, and on June 10, 1772, a group of Providence merchants lured a British customs ship (there to collect taxes) called the *Gaspee* into Narragansett Bay and set it on fire. The *Gaspee*'s commander was shot and wounded during the colonists' attack. These events in Rhode Island marked the first acts of colonial rebellion against Great Britain.

Rebellion flared with the burning of the British ship *Gaspee*.

Providence

Warwick Neck
Lighthouse

Cranston

1. Providence: population 178,042

Founded in 1636, Providence is the state capital and one of the oldest cities in the United States. In the 1990s, the mayor spearheaded improvements such as the creation of Waterplace Park and the Bank of America Skating Rink.

2. Warwick: population 82,672

Founded in 1642, Warwick was decimated during King Philip's War (1675–76) and was the site of the Gaspee Affair, a prelude to the American Revolution. Today, it is a place for residents to relax at freshwater or saltwater beaches.

3. Cranston: population 80,387

Created in 1754 as Pawtuxet, it became Cranston on March 10, 1910. Cranston was named one of the "100 Best Places to Live" in the United States by Money magazine in 2006.

4. Pawtucket: population 71,148

Pawtucket was founded in 1671, and it was a major contributor of cotton textiles during the American Industrial Revolution. Slater Mill, built in 1793 in downtown Pawtucket, was the first fully mechanized cotton-spinning mill in America.

5. East Providence: population 47,037

East Providence has its origins in land purchases in 1641 and 1661, and was incorporated in 1862 as a city from "Old Seekonk." The city is actually made up of the three villages of East Providence Center, Riverside, and Rumford.

6. Woonsocket: population 41,186

Woonsocket was not incorporated until 1888 when the six villages of Bernon, Globe, Hamlet, Jenckesville, Social, and Woonsocket Falls, were joined. It is home to Autumnfest, an annual cultural festival held on Columbus Day Weekend.

7. Coventry: population 35,014

Coventry was settled in the early eighteenth century. Farmhouses from that era can be found scattered around the town, and many are still private residences. On the eastern side of town, homes from the nineteenth century can be found.

8. Cumberland: population 33,506

Cumberland is the northeasternmost town in Rhode Island. It was settled in 1635 and incorporated in 1746. It is home to the headquarters and original 1955 location of Ann & Hope discount stores, which claims to be the first chain of discount department stores in America.

9. North Providence: population 32,078

Established in 1636 and incorporated as a town in 1765, North Providence originally included parts of what are today the cities of Providence and Pawtucket. It is the smallest town by area (5.9 sq. miles/9.5 km) in the smallest state (1,216 sq. miles/1,957 km).

10. South Kingstown: population 30,639

South Kingstown was formed in 1722 when the former Kings Towne was split into two parts, the other being North Kingstown. South Kingstown was incorporated in 1723, and was named for Charles II of England.

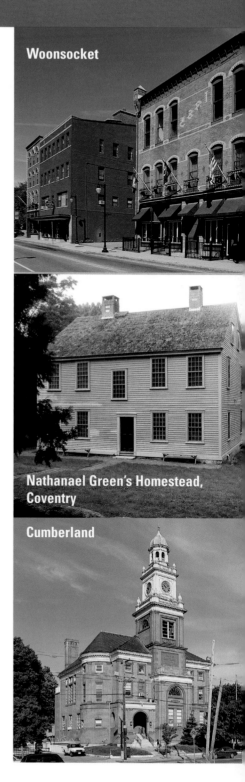

Woonsocket

Nathanael Green's Homestead, Coventry

Cumberland

The American Revolution

In the spring of 1775, colonists in Massachusetts Bay fought British troops at Lexington and Concord, beginning the American Revolution. Rhode Island immediately sent troops to help its neighbor fight the British. In June, George Washington was appointed the leader of the Continental Army that would bring together soldiers from all of the thirteen colonies.

Washington was appointed by the Second Continental Congress, which included representatives from the thirteen colonies. Rhode Island's delegates urged the formation of an American fleet, and the Continental Navy was established in October 1775. Stephen and Esek Hopkins, brothers from Rhode Island, helped create the Continental Navy. Esek Hopkins became its first commander-in-chief.

On May 4, 1776, Rhode Island became the first New England colony to declare independence from Great Britain. Two months later, on July 4, 1776, delegates from all thirteen colonies, at the Continental Congress, approved the Declaration of Independence, stating that "these United Colonies are, and of Right ought to be, Free and Independent States."

The American Revolution included many battles throughout the colonies, and Rhode Island soldiers took part in the fighting. Residents in the colony who supported independence also provided supplies, money, and food for the troops. In August 1778, one of the largest land battles of the American Revolution known as the Battle of Rhode Island took place near Newport. General Nathanael Greene, a Rhode Islander, led American troops during the battle.

Also fighting in the Battle of Rhode Island was a group of soldiers called the Black Regiment of Rhode Island. They formed the first African-American army unit. The soldiers were made up of more than 120 black men, including about one hundred enslaved Africans.

Greene played a key role in the final British defeat. Under his leadership, American troops in the South forced a British army led by General Cornwallis to retreat to Yorktown, Virginia, in 1781.

First to Arrive

In 1623, an English minister named William Blackstone, displeased with the Church of England, joined an expedition sailing to present-day Massachusetts. Then, in 1635, Blackstone became the first European to settle in the area that is now Rhode Island. The Blackstone River in northeastern Rhode Island is named after him.

Major General Nathanael Greene was one of George Washington's most trusted officers.

There, George Washington and his troops, supported by French forces, trapped and attacked Cornwallis's army and forced the British to surrender.

In 1783, the former thirteen colonies signed a peace agreement with Great Britain called the Treaty of Paris, in which Britain officially accepted American independence. In 1787, the Constitution of the United States of America was drafted at a convention in Philadelphia. The document outlined how the U.S. government would operate and what powers it would have. Each state had to ratify (approve) the Constitution.

Rhode Islanders were concerned about giving up too much power to the federal government, however. They refused to ratify the Constitution until it included additional rights that would protect individual liberties and limit federal authority. Finally, the U.S. Congress approved the first ten amendments to the Constitution, called the Bill of Rights. On May 29, 1790, Rhode Island approved the U.S. Constitution. It was the last of the original thirteen colonies to do so.

The Industrial Revolution Begins

In the late 1700s and into the 1800s, Rhode Island's **economy** boomed due to the Industrial Revolution, when manufacturing became a major **industry** in the state. A Providence merchant who had been operating a mill that spun cotton in Pawtucket visited Great Britain and witnessed how British cotton mills used water-powered machines to spin cotton into thread. These machines allowed the British mills to produce goods faster

and cheaper. The merchant wished to know how to build and run such machines, but British mill owners guarded their operations against foreign competition. In fact, anyone who worked in a water-powered mill in Great Britain was forbidden to leave the country.

However, one mill worker did manage to slip out undetected. Samuel Slater disguised himself as a farmer, boarded a ship, and ended up in Pawtucket in 1790. Slater worked with the merchant, Moses Brown, to recreate a water-powered mill similar to those in Great Britain. The rolling Blackstone River was the perfect source for a waterwheel. In 1793, Slater created the first water-powered cotton mill in the United States.

Within a few years, other mills sprang up along Rhode Island's many rivers. Textiles (cloth) became a leading industry for the state. The use of water to power mills was also applied to other industries. Pawtucket's David Wilkinson developed a water-powered mill to manufacture metal tools and equipment, shifting the economy from farming and sea trading to manufacturing.

In 1794, two brothers, Nehemiah and Seril Dodge, started making costume jewelry in Providence. They found a way to cover cheaper metals with better-looking and more expensive metals. With this innovation, Rhode Island entered the jewelry industry. By 1824, Providence had become the jewelry-making capital of North America.

In the 1830s, silversmith Jabez Gorham began manufacturing sterling silver. It is a pure silver melted with another metal, often copper, to make it stronger. At first, Gorham made spoons, thimbles, and jewelry. In time, his son, John, made the Gorham Manufacturing Company into the largest sterling silver manufacturer in the world. Many U.S. presidents have served their guests using Gorham silverware.

From the 1840s through the 1850s, railroad lines began to cross through Rhode Island. The railroads helped connect Rhode Island to other states, making it cheaper for Rhode Island's factories to ship their products around the country, which made manufacturing more profitable.

As word of the state's economic prosperity spread, it began to attract people from other countries seeking better opportunities. Soon, a steady stream of **immigrants** made their way into the state. Rhode Island's population skyrocketed from just under seventy thousand in 1800 to almost 148,000 in 1850.

The Dorr Rebellion

In 1841, a Providence attorney named Thomas Dorr tried to change the state's outdated charter, starting a movement known as the Dorr Rebellion. Dorr and his supporters drafted a new constitution that extended voting rights to all adult males who lived within the state. His supporters held their own statewide election and elected Dorr as their governor in 1842. However, he was arrested, convicted of treason, and sentenced to life in prison, though he was released after serving only a year. The Dorr Rebellion led to a revised state constitution in 1843. The change allowed males, including African Americans, who were born in the United States to vote without owning property if they could pay a $1 poll tax.

Thomas Dorr fought to expand voting rights in Rhode Island.

Colonel Ambrose E. Burnside (center) and the
Rhode Island Brigade were among the first units formed to fight in the Civil War.

The Civil War

Not long after Abraham Lincoln was elected the sixteenth U.S. president in 1860, the Civil War (1861–1865) broke out. This conflict bitterly divided Northern and Southern states who disagreed on slavery and other issues. Most Northerners opposed slavery while many Southerners believed they had the right to own slaves.

Southern states feared Lincoln's election would lead to restrictions on or even the abolition of slavery. By early 1861, eleven Southern states decided to break away from the United States and formed a new government called the Confederate States of America. The other states went to war to bring the Confederate states back into the Union.

Rhode Island manufacturers had been buying a great deal of cotton from Southern states to keep their textile mills running, so they did not want to fight against the Confederacy. Eventually, though, Rhode Island contributed more than twenty-four thousand troops to the Union army. The state's factories and farms provided supplies and food for Union troops.

After years of fighting and the loss of hundreds of thousands of lives, the Confederacy surrendered in 1865. Then the Thirteenth Amendment to the U.S. Constitution was adopted, outlawing slavery throughout the United States.

The Gilded Age

Rhode Island's economy and population continued to grow after the Civil War. The state's textile mills produced thread, yarn, cotton shirts, and other goods, which were then shipped to countries all over the world. Rhode Island's jewelry and metal products industries were also flourishing.

This economic prosperity set the stage for a period in the late 1800s known as the Gilded Age. During this time, many of the country's richest families, such as the Astor, Vanderbilt, Morgan, and Belmont families, chose to spend summers in Newport. Members of these elite families, most of them based in New York, were famous business leaders who made huge fortunes in manufacturing, transportation, and banking. They built stunning seaside mansions located on Newport's Bellevue Avenue, which have been designated National Historic Landmarks.

Other mansions, such as Hammersmith Farm, built in 1887, have been turned into private residences. The wedding reception of Jacqueline Bouvier and John F. Kennedy was held at Hammersmith Farm in 1953. Jacqueline spent summers as a child in the twenty-eight-room Victorian mansion. During President Kennedy's time in office, Hammersmith Farm became known as the Summer White House due to his frequent visits.

The Twentieth Century

In the 1900s, immigrants were drawn to Rhode Island's industrial success. Most of the immigrants came from Italy, Ireland, Great Britain, Portugal, Russia, Poland, and French-speaking areas of Canada. In Providence alone, the population soared from about fifty-five thousand in 1865 to more than 175,000 in 1900. By 1925, Providence's population reached an all-time peak of 267,918.

Factory workers put in long hours in buildings that were cold during the winter and hot during the summer. Some of the machinery was dangerous and workers often suffered injuries, and even children went to work in factories and mills to help their families earn money. In the early 1900s, some reforms were made to try to protect workers from the most dangerous conditions. But the average working family still had a very difficult time making a living.

When the United States entered World War I in 1917, Rhode Island provided supplies and troops. By the time the war ended in 1918, several of Rhode Island's industries were no longer as profitable. Many of the state's textile companies had moved their mills to southern states where laborers would work for lower wages.

Things grew worse for the Ocean State during the Great Depression, which began when the stock market collapsed in 1929. Many people lost all of their money. Businesses closed and thousands of people were put out of work. Rhode Island's once-thriving textile industry had practically disappeared.

The economy began to improve during World War II. American factories reopened in 1941, manufacturing goods for the war effort. Rhode Island's factories produced ammunition, chemicals, machinery, electronics, and other war materials. U.S. troops used metal shelters called Quonset huts (developed at the Quonset Point Naval Air Station in Rhode Island) for storage, housing, and medical centers. About ninety-two thousand Rhode Islanders served in the armed forces in World War II.

Once the war was over, Rhode Island's difficult economic times returned. Unemployment became alarmingly high. To replace the declining textile industry, efforts were made to attract other businesses. Companies specializing in electronic equipment, plastics, machinery, chemicals, health care products, and toys began moving into the state.

In the twenty-first century, Rhode Island remains a popular vacation spot. But like the rest of the country, the state suffered difficult times after a severe nationwide economic recession began at the end of 2007. Many people lost their jobs. By June 2014, Rhode Island was tied with Mississippi for the highest unemployment rate (7.9 percent) of any U.S. state.

Old factories in Providence's former jewelry district have been converted into grand buildings in the new Knowledge District. Rhode Island's focus now is on recruiting jobs in health care and other "knowledge-based" industries. Brown University recently opened a $45-million medical school here.

Narragansett Bay remained a training site for submarine crews after World War II.

10 KEY DATES IN STATE HISTORY

1. **1636**
Puritan leader Roger Williams establishes Providence, the first settlement in Rhode Island, after being banished from the Massachusetts Bay Colony.

2. **1663**
King Charles II of England grants Providence Plantations a new royal charter, allowing it more self-government and religious freedom.

3. **December 2, 1763**
Touro Synagogue, the oldest synagogue in the present-day United States, is dedicated in Newport.

4. **May 4, 1776**
Rhode Island becomes the first colony to declare independence from Great Britain.

5. **1793**
Samuel Slater builds the first successful factory in the United States, helping to launch the Industrial Revolution in the country. The water-powered mill, dedicated to cotton-spinning until 1829, is located in Pawtucket.

6. **May 19, 1842**
Dorr Rebellion begins with an unsuccessful assault commanded by Thomas W. Dorr on the arsenal in Providence. The rebellion was begun over voting rights for white males who did not own land.

7. **1930**
America's Cup races moved to Newport, where they would remain until 1983.

8. **September 12, 1953**
Future president John F. Kennedy marries Jacqueline Bouvier in St. Mary's Church, the state's oldest Roman Catholic Parish.

9. **Feb. 20, 2003**
A fire in a nightclub in West Warwick, set off by a heavy metal band's pyrotechnics, kills one hundred patrons.

10. **August 26, 2011**
Although Hurricane Irene knocks out power to half of the state's residents, hurricane barriers prevent flooding.

Sail boat repair is a skill handed down by Rhode Islander's to their children.

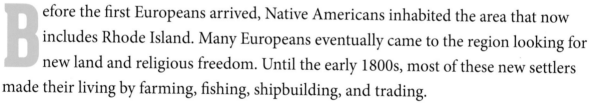

The People

Before the first Europeans arrived, Native Americans inhabited the area that now includes Rhode Island. Many Europeans eventually came to the region looking for new land and religious freedom. Until the early 1800s, most of these new settlers made their living by farming, fishing, shipbuilding, and trading.

As new technologies developed, manufacturing became the center of Rhode Island's economy. Factories sprang up quickly in the state's major cities. With the increase in factories came the need for more people to work in them. Rhode Island became a magnet for European and other immigrants, attracting a steady stream of people from a wide variety of backgrounds and nationalities.

The Irish began immigrating to Rhode Island in the 1820s. They worked in factories and helped build the state's railroads.

In 1824, women textile mill workers in Pawtucket went on strike to protest attempts by the mill owners to lower the workers' pay and require a longer workday. During a strike, people stop working in an attempt to force their employer to meet their demands. The Pawtucket work stoppage is believed to be the first strike by women workers in the United States. The strike was successful, forcing the mill owners to withdraw their wage cuts and increase of hours.

During the 1860s, people from Canada as well as Germany, Sweden, Portugal, and the Cape Verde Islands off the west coast of Africa made their way to the state.

Many of the Portuguese immigrants were skilled sailors. When they arrived in Newport and Providence during the 1860s, they found work on Rhode Island's whaling ships. Descendants of these workers still live in areas such as Providence's Fox Point community.

A popular tourist attraction in Newport is a seventy-room summer "cottage" known as the Breakers. New York tycoon Cornelius Vanderbilt II built the Breakers, Newport's grandest mansion, in the 1890s. His family made its fortune in steamships and railroads. Thirty-three of the mansion's rooms were required for Vanderbilt's servants alone. The main rooms are filled with finely polished marble and alabaster, glistening crystal chandeliers, velvet draperies and cushions, and walls covered with gold leaf. The estate offers amazing views of the Atlantic Ocean.

In the 1890s and early 1900s, immigrants arrived from Italy, Greece, Russia, Poland, Syria, Lithuania, Armenia, Lebanon, and Ukraine. In the 1970s, many Hispanics began settling in Rhode Island. They have come from Puerto Rico and from such Spanish-speaking countries as Colombia, Mexico, the Dominican Republic, and Guatemala. In addition, Asians have moved to the state from countries such as Vietnam, Cambodia, and China. No matter where they are from, Rhode Islanders bring their cultures, religions, and traditions to enrich the state.

A large number of French Canadians moved to the northern city of Woonsocket during the mid-1800s. They left Quebec in Canada to work in Woonsocket's mills and factories, producing rubber, cotton cloth, and machines. Many of their descendants are still in Woonsocket. They often speak to one another in French. French Canadians make up Woonsocket's largest ethnic group today. Woonsocket's Museum of Work and Culture tells the story of French Canadian immigrants who came to work in the city.

Father of Founding Fathers

Thomas Jefferson of Virginia and John Adams of Massachusetts are known as two of the founding fathers of the United States. However, they acknowledged that Roger Williams was the originator of these principles spoken of in The First Amendment to the constitution: freedom of religion, freedom of speech, and freedom of public assembly.

Who Rhode Islanders Are

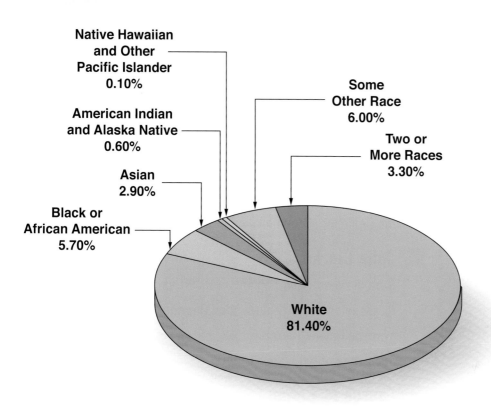

Native Hawaiian and Other Pacific Islander 0.10%

American Indian and Alaska Native 0.60%

Asian 2.90%

Black or African American 5.70%

Some Other Race 6.00%

Two or More Races 3.30%

White 81.40%

Total Population 1,052,567

Hispanic or Latino (of any race):
- 130,655 people (12.40%)

Note: The pie chart shows the racial breakdown of the state's population based on the categories used by the U.S. Bureau of the Census. The Census Bureau reports information for Hispanics or Latinos separately, since they may be of any race. Percentages in the pie chart may not add to 100 because of rounding.

Source: U.S. Bureau of the Census, 2010 Census

Rhode Island's Population Today

According to the 2010 U.S. Census, Rhode Island had 1,052,567 residents as of April 1 of that year. Among the states, Rhode Island ranks forty-third in population. Rhode Island is the second most crowded, or densely populated, state in the country, however. An average of 1,018 people live in each square mile of land (393 people per sq. km).

A lack of job opportunities has affected Rhode Island's population. In fact, Rhode Island is one of the slowest-growing states. Its population in 2010 had inched up by just 4,248 residents—a 0.4 percent increase—since 2000. The only state that grew slower than Rhode Island from 2000 to 2010 was Michigan.

Most people in Rhode Island reside in urban areas. Rhode Island's five most populous cities are Providence, Warwick, Cranston, Pawtucket, and East Providence. These cities are located in the eastern section of the state. The rest of Rhode Islanders are spread out among the small, outlying rural communities.

Kady Brownell

George M. Cohan

Viola Davis

1. Kady Brownell

When Bronwell's husband joined a military unit called the Rhode Island Infantry at the outbreak of the Civil War, she signed up as well. She carried the flag into battle, helped injured soldiers, and was often referred to as a Daughter of the Regiment. Brownell died in 1915.

2. John Clarke

Born in Westhorpe, England in 1609, the co-founder of the Rhode Island colony persuaded Charles II of England to grant its Royal Charter in 1663, and wrote it with an explicit guarantee of religious freedom.

3. George M. Cohan

Thanks to George M. Cohan, musical comedy became a popular form of entertainment in America during the 1920s and 1930s. Born in Providence in 1878, Cohan was the first songwriter to be awarded the Congressional Medal of Honor for his World War I song, "Over There."

4. Viola Davis

Actress Viola Davis moved with her family to Central Falls, Rhode Island as an infant. She has won two Tony Awards for her theater work, and was nominated for Academy Awards for her roles in *Doubt* and *The Help*.

5. The Farrelly Brothers

Bobby and Peter were raised in Cumberland. They have written, directed, and produced many films, including the blockbuster *Dumb and Dumber*. They received 1999 PGA Golden Laurel Awards for *There's Something About Mary*.

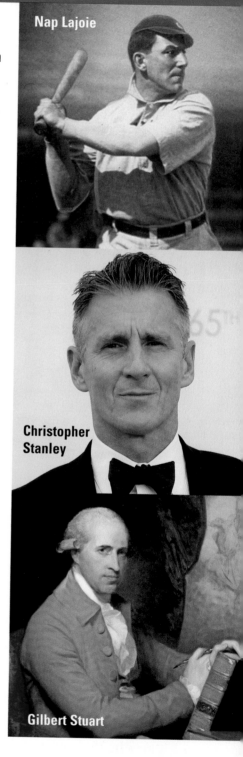

Nap Lajoie

Christopher Stanley

Gilbert Stuart

6. Napoleon Lajoie

Hall of Fame baseball player Napoleon "Nap" Lajoie was born in Woonsocket in 1874. Second baseman for the Philadelphia Phillies, the Philadelphia Athletics, and the Cleveland Indians, he was considered one of the early twentieth century's greatest players. Lajoie died in 1959.

7. Ida Lewis

Lewis' father was a lighthouse keeper. When he became ill in the 1850s, she took over the responsibilities of maintaining Lime Rock Light Station in Newport Harbor, serving until her death in 1911. Lime Rock was eventually renamed the Ida Lewis Lighthouse.

8. Sherwood Spring

Sherwood "Woody" Spring of Harmony, Rhode Island was born in 1944. A retired United States Army Colonel and astronaut, he has logged 165 hours in space.

9. Christopher Stanley

Born and raised in Providence, Christopher Stanley became interested in acting as a teenager. Since 1986, he has worked in both film and television with notable performances in critically acclaimed shows *NYPD Blue*, *Mad Men*, and movies *Argo* and *Zero Dark Thirty*.

10. Gilbert Stuart

Born in Saunderstown in 1755, Stuart is considered the Father of American Portraiture, having painted more than a thousand portraits until his death in 1828. His portrait of George Washington is featured on the U.S. one-dollar bill.

Rhode Island is the second most densely populated state.

Becoming More Diverse

Most Rhode Islanders trace their ancestry to Europe. Over the years, however, people with other backgrounds have settled in the state.

Hispanic Americans make up the state's largest and fastest-growing cultural group. In 2000, there were 90,820 Hispanic Rhode Islanders. They made up 8.7 percent of the state's population. That number increased to 130,655 in 2010, when Hispanics made

Naval Torpedo Station

During World War II, many Rhode Islanders went to work in the state's factories. Women helped produce about seventeen thousand torpedoes at the Naval Torpedo Station on Newport's Goat Island.

up 12.4 percent of the population. That is an increase of more than 40 percent. Many of Rhode Island's Hispanic residents live in communities in Providence, the state's capital and largest city. Today, African Americans comprise almost 6 percent of the state's population. The state's Asian population is nearly 3 percent.

Native American

Before European settlement, the region's population was Native American. Today, however, Native Americans number only about six thousand. About 2,400 belong to the Narragansett group. The tribe's headquarters are located on a reservation in Charlestown in southern Rhode Island.

The Narragansett Indians sued the state in the 1970s to regain their lands. They were awarded about 1,800 acres (700 hectares) near Charlestown. In 1983, they gained federal recognition as the Narragansett Indian Tribe of Rhode Island.

On the reservation, the tribe keeps its heritage alive through traditional crafts, songs, storytelling, an annual powwow, and other celebrations. People can also visit the Royal Indian Burial Ground in Charlestown. It is the resting place of many Narragansett *sachems* (chiefs) and their families.

St. Anne's Church was built for the French Canadian population in Woonsocket.

Innovative schools, such as the International Charter School in Pawtucket, teach in English, Spanish, and Portuguese.

Education

Education is important to Rhode Islanders. The state's public education system began in the 1820s. Today, many people work for the state's school system.

Some of Rhode Island's universities are also among the state's largest employers. The main campus of the state's public university—the University of Rhode Island (URI)—is located in Kingston. URI began as an agricultural school in 1888. Today, more than nineteen thousand students are enrolled there. The school has one of the nation's leading centers for ocean research and exploration.

Established in Newport in 1747, the Redwood Library and Athenaeum is the first library in Rhode Island and the oldest

We're Number 3

Founded in 1764, Brown is the third-oldest college in New England and the seventh-oldest college in the United States. The institution, originally located in Warren and called the College of Rhode Island, moved to Providence in 1770. It was renamed Brown University in 1804 after businessman and 1786 graduate Nicholas Brown gave a gift totaling $5,000. Brown University began admitting women in 1891. More recently, Emma Watson, who rose to fame as Hermione in the Harry Potter films, has also attended Brown.

lending library in the United States. In a lending library, members pay fees to access materials. One of Redwood's most famous librarians, Ezra Stiles (1727–1795), helped found Brown University in Providence. He later became the president of Yale University in New Haven, Connecticut.

Providence is home to several other colleges and universities. Brown graduates include Horace Mann from the class of 1819, considered the father of American public education, and Charles Evans Hughes, who served as U.S. Supreme Court chief justice from 1930 to 1941. Other schools in Providence include Providence College, Johnson and Wales University (known for its culinary arts program), and the Rhode Island School of Design (RISD). RISD's Museum of Art contains an impressive collection of pieces from around the world as well as the work of African American landscape artist Edward Mitchell Bannister, who painted in Rhode Island during the 1800s.

Located in Bristol is Roger Williams University. The school was named after Rhode Island's founder. Newport is home to Salve Regina University and the U.S. Naval War College, which trains naval officers.

Brown University was founded in 1764.

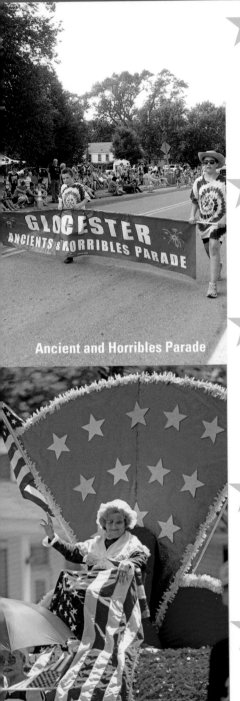

Ancient and Horribles Parade

Bristol Fourth of July parade

1. Ancient and Horribles Parade

Since 1927, the Ancient and Horribles Parade has taken place each Independence Day in the town of Glocester. People wear wild and wacky outfits and decorate their cars. These types of parades date back to the 1870s or earlier in small New England towns.

2. Autumnfest

Since 1977, the northern city of Woonsocket has hosted this huge October event. The celebration includes amusement park rides and games, arts and crafts displays, spectacular fireworks, musical entertainment, and a parade.

3. Black Ships Festival

In 1854, Rhode Island's Commodore Matthew C. Perry negotiated a trade treaty with Japan. Previously, foreign ships not permitted to enter Japan were called Black Ships—or *kurofune* in Japanese. This Newport festival in July honors the relations that Perry established with Japan.

4. Bristol Fourth of July Celebration

Since 1785, Bristol has held the oldest continuous Fourth of July celebration in the United States. The popular event includes a parade, pageants, food, music, dancing, games, displays, and fireworks.

5. Gaspee Days Colonial Encampment

Each June, the city of Warwick commemorates the burning of the British customs ship *Gaspee* by Rhode Island colonists in 1772 with several events. At the encampment, visitors reenact military life during Rhode Island's colonial period.

6. Indoor Powwow

Held in Warwick, this November powwow displays Rhode Island's rich Native American heritage. In addition to drumming, singing, and intertribal dances, there are arts, crafts, and storytelling.

7. International Quahog Festival

Clam lovers flock to this August festival, which pays tribute to the quahog clam. In addition to quahog chowder, visitors can try clam cakes, a stuffed, baked clam called a "stuffy," quahog chili, fried quahogs, and quahogs on the half shell.

8. Newport Jazz Festival

The country's first jazz festival took place in Newport in 1954. The summer event attracts people from all over the world. Past performers have included jazz greats such as Louis Armstrong, Ella Fitzgerald, Duke Ellington, and Miles Davis.

9. Scituate Art Festival

This Columbus Day weekend event takes place in the picturesque town of Scituate surrounded by beautiful fall foliage. It draws close to three hundred exhibitors specializing in painting, sculpture, antiques, and crafts.

10. Washington County Fair

Held in rural Richmond, this mid-August event is Rhode Island's largest agricultural fair. Among the many attractions are the farm museum, tractor pulls, crafts, New England food, and performances by country music artists.

International Quahog Festival

Scituate Art Festival

The statue on top of the State House dome is known as "Independent Man."

How the Government Works

R hode Island once had five state capitals—one for each county. In 1854, the number was reduced to two—Providence and Newport. In 1900, Providence became the sole capital.

Rhode Island's current state constitution was adopted in 1843. Since then, it has been changed, or amended, more than forty times. Amendments to the constitution must be approved first by a majority vote in both houses of the state legislature, followed by a majority vote of the people in an election.

A state constitution describes how a state's government is organized and what powers the government has. A state constitution also limits the powers of government in order to protect the rights of individuals. Like the U.S. Constitution, the Rhode Island constitution divides its government into three separate branches to balance the power of each branch. The executive branch carries out state laws, the legislative branch makes new laws or changes existing ones, and the judicial branch interprets laws.

The Rhode Island State House has a design similar to the U.S. Capitol's, with a central dome between two wings.

State Government

A governor, elected to a four-year term, heads the state. Rhode Island is one of the few states that does not have an official governor's residence. Rhode Island's legislature is called the general assembly. It is made up of two houses, or chambers, a senate and a house of representatives. Senators and representatives represent specific regions of the state.

The state government is responsible for issues that affect the state. The job of state officials includes drafting, approving, and enforcing laws, as well as managing state budgets. The state government also handles issues with other states, as well as with the federal government in Washington, DC.

Rhode Island's state government is centered in its capital, Providence. State lawmakers meet inside the capitol, called the Rhode Island State House. The governor, lieutenant governor, secretary of state, general treasurer, and other officials work here as well.

Building began on the Rhode Island State House in 1895. Inside the building is a vault that contains the Royal Charter of 1663 from King Charles II of England. The charter guaranteed Rhode Island's settlers freedom of religion and freedom to govern their own colony. Hanging in the Rhode Island State House is the famous painting of George Washington by Rhode Island's Gilbert Stuart.

Representation in Washington, DC

At the national level, Rhode Island has representatives in both houses of the U.S. Congress. Each state elects two U.S. senators, who serve six-year terms. There is no limit on the number of terms a U.S. senator can serve. A state's population determines the number of people that it sends to the U.S. House of Representatives. Rhode Islanders elect two representatives to the House. They serve two-year terms and can be reelected an unlimited number of times.

Local Government

Rhode Island is divided into five counties—Providence, Kent, Washington, Bristol, and Newport. There is, however, no county government. The main units of local government within the state are its thirty-nine municipalities. They are made up of eight cities and thirty-one towns. The majority of these municipalities are presided over by a mayor and a city or town council.

As in other states, many towns in Rhode Island hold annual town meetings. These meetings originated during the colonial era, and all eligible voters can attend. At these sessions, voters can approve local spending, pass laws, and even elect local officials.

The state seal adorns the floor of the State House.

Branches of Government

Executive

The governor heads the executive branch. The governor carries out the laws that the legislative branch passes and is elected every four years. The governor may serve only two terms in a row. Other executive branch officials include the lieutenant governor (who takes over if the governor can no longer serve), attorney general, secretary of state, and general treasurer. Each of these officials is voted into office to serve a four-year term. Like the governor, these elected officials cannot serve more than two terms in a row.

Legislative

Rhode Island's legislative branch is called the general assembly. It is made up of a senate with thirty-eight members and a house of representatives with seventy-five members. Members of both houses earn their jobs through popular elections, and each serves a two-year term. Rhode Island's general assembly is responsible for making the state's laws and approving people nominated by the governor to be justices of the state's supreme court.

Judicial

Rhode Island's judicial branch interprets and applies the state's laws. The state's highest court is the supreme court. It is made up of a chief justice and four associate justices who serve life terms. The superior court is the state's main trial court. It consists of twenty-two judges whom the governor chooses with the senate's approval. In addition, Rhode Island has family, district, municipal, and probate courts. The governor, with the consent of the senate, appoints these judges. More serious criminal and civil cases are sent to the superior court, which also hears appeals of district court decisions.

How a Bill Becomes a Law

State laws often start out as the ideas of concerned residents. Any Rhode Islander can talk to his or her state legislators about issues that affect the state and its residents. If a resident—or a group of residents—has a suggestion for a new law, it can be presented to a state legislator. Often, the legislator will develop the idea into a bill (a proposed law). The bill is then presented to the legislator's chamber of the general assembly.

If the legislator is a senator, the bill is brought first to the senate. If the legislator is a state representative, the bill is brought to the house of representatives.

The bill gets a specific number to identify it. The numbered bill then goes to a committee of legislators for review. The committee members read and discuss the bill. If they agree with it, they can recommend that the bill is passed as it is. If the bill is not

The house gallery provides residents with the opportunity to see how the legislature works.

recommended, it does not move forward. The committee can also make changes, refer the bill to another committee, or recommend that the discussion of the bill should be postponed. The committee may also present the bill to fellow legislators without comment.

If the bill is recommended for passage, it is discussed by the full senate or full house. Changes may be made or the bill might remain the same. If the legislators of one house approve the bill, it goes to the other chamber for approval. Once there, the bill follows the same process until it is approved. If the senate and the house approve two different versions of the same bill, a conference committee that includes members of both houses meets to resolve the differences. The committee ultimately creates a final version of the bill for approval by both chambers of the general assembly.

A bill that has been approved by both houses in exactly the same form is then sent to the governor. The governor can approve the bill by signing it, and the bill becomes a law. He or she can also allow the bill to become law without signing it. If the governor disagrees with the bill, he or she can veto (reject) it. Even if a bill is vetoed, it still has a chance to become law if three-fifths of the members of both houses of the legislature vote again to approve it. This is called overriding the governor's veto.

In Their Own Words

"I have the philosophy that one person can make a difference. Especially when one person is joined by another and another."–Claudine Schneider, U.S. Representative

POLITICAL ★ FIGURES
FROM RHODE ISLAND

★ Lincoln Davenport Chafee: Governor, 2011-2015

Sworn in as the seventy-fourth Governor of Rhode Island in January 2011, Chafee had previously served as a United States Senator and as Warwick's mayor. In 2007, he left the Republican Party to become an independent, and in 2013 joined the Democratic Party. On May 1, 2013, Chafee signed a bill that legalized same-sex marriage in Rhode Island.

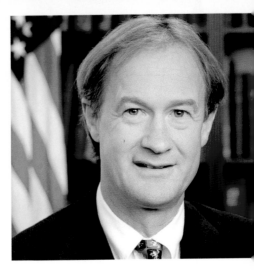

★ Arthur Fenner: Governor, 1745-1790

Fenner served as the fourth Governor of Rhode Island from 1790 until his death in 1805, while he was still in office. While Fenner was a prominent Country Party (Anti-federalist) leader, he was governor of Rhode Island when it became the last of the thirteen states to ratify the Constitution on May 29, 1790.

★ Claiborne de Borda Pell: U.S. Senator, 1961-1997

Pell was the longest serving U.S. Senator from Rhode Island, serving six terms from 1961 to 1997. He is best known as the sponsor of the Pell Grant, which provides financial aid funding to American college students. He also participated in the 1945 San Francisco conference that drafted the United Nations Charter.

Contacting Lawmakers

Rhode Islanders can take an active role in government and contact their representative and senator about issues of concern. To find contact information for Rhode Island's state legislators, visit:

sos.ri.gov/vic

Enter your street and zip code or city or town to find your senator and representative.

To find out who represents an area in the federal government in Washington, DC as a congressman or senator, visit:

www.ri.gov/links/?tags=house+of+representatives

www.senate.gov/general/contact_information/senators_cfm.cfm?State=RI

The Urban Pond Procession in Providence.

Making a Difference

In 2007, artist Holly Ewald was hired on behalf of the health department to make new signs to warn people of the health hazards connected with the polluted Mashapaug Pond in Providence. The existing warning signs were in English, and non-English speaking families, particularly Spanish and Cambodian families, were eating fish from the pond.

Ewald decided to draw attention to the pond, and came up with the idea of a celebration called the Urban Pond Procession. She worked for a year with schools, the Cambodian temple, and other groups to create colorful costumes for the parade.

Government officials were ecstatic with the response, and multilingual signs around the pond today reflect the designs created by the school children.

Ewald has attracted help from artists, scientists, educators, and residents who share a goal of promoting the health of urban ponds. The annual procession has started other projects around the pond. Remediation efforts are under way, and when the work is done the land will be given to the Providence Parks Department.

Farmers sell their produce at the Hope Street Farmers Market on Saturdays in Providence.

Making a Living

Throughout Rhode Island's history, its people have found ways to survive on the land. For many years, farming, raising livestock, and fishing in the rivers, bays, and the ocean were major ways that residents made a living. Over time, however, manufacturing and service industries grew in importance. Service industries are those in which workers provide a service to others rather than produce goods. An important service industry in Rhode Island today involves meeting the needs of the many tourists who visit the state each year.

In the twenty-first century, Rhode Islanders are also focused on bringing emerging jobs in biotechnology and other high-tech fields to the state to bolster its economy.

Manufacturing

After Samuel Slater built his water-powered cotton mill in Pawtucket, Rhode Island quickly became a manufacturing giant. Textile mills were soon lining the state's rivers. During the entire nineteenth and early twentieth centuries, manufacturing was the most profitable industry in Rhode Island. More than half the state's workforce was employed in factories and mills. Today, however, there are fewer manufacturing jobs in the state. Although many factories have closed or relocated, the manufacturing industry still employs about fifty-seven thousand people. Those workers make up nearly 12 percent of the state's labor force.

Copper wire is among the metal products manufactured in the state.

Rhode Island manufactures metal products such as nuts, bolts, wires, tools, and machine parts. Other leading manufactured products include chemicals, plastics, textiles, transportation equipment, electronic equipment, and scientific equipment—particularly medical and surgical products. Yachts, boats, and some submarine parts are also made in Rhode Island. In addition, Rhode Island is known for producing jewelry and silverware. Providence is home to many jewelry manufacturing companies.

In the mid-1700s, Newport was a major furniture-making center. Two of colonial America's best-known furniture makers—the Townsend and Goddard families—lived and worked in Easton's Point, a Quaker neighborhood in Newport. Many of their best-known pieces were made from mahogany wood imported from the West Indies.

Today, Newport furniture from the eighteenth century is very valuable. Many world-class museums include Townsend-Goddard pieces in their collections. In 1989, a mahogany Goddard desk and bookcase made in the 1760s sold for $12.1 million. It was the highest price ever paid for a piece of furniture.

Agriculture, Livestock, and Fishing

Farming, raising livestock, and fishing make up a very small part of Rhode Island's economy today. Less than 1 percent of Rhode Island's labor force works in these areas. The number of farms in the state grew between 2007 and 2012; at that time Rhode Island had

1,243 farms. The number of farms in the state increased by almost half in a decade; this came at a time when farm totals decreased in the rest of the country.

Rhode Island's top farm products are nursery and greenhouse plants. These include flowering plants, Christmas trees, grass sod, and decorative trees and shrubs. Milk and other dairy products are other main agricultural commodities. Rhode Island farm crops include potatoes, sweet corn, tomatoes, and squash. Rhode Island's orchards grow fruits such as apples, peaches, pears, and berries.

Farmers raise different types of livestock, including dairy cows, hogs, and hens. The products that come from the livestock are often processed or prepared in the state. The Rhode Island Red (the state bird) is a special breed of chicken raised in Little Compton.

Commercial fishing is not as large an industry as it once was. But fishing boats in towns and villages such as Galilee along the Narragansett Bay bring in flounder, cod, tuna, squid, scallops, and whiting. Rhode Island fishers also harvest clams and lobsters.

Rhode Island's seafood industry is threatened by pollution in Narragansett Bay, where most of the state's fishing takes place. State sewage treatment plants that were built in the 1800s are no longer effective. After a heavy rainfall, water tends to fill up the treatment plants, causing an overflow of sewage into the bay. This sewage is harming the fish and other sea creatures, affecting the state's fishing industry, but environmental groups and concerned citizens are working to reduce pollution in the bay.

Commercial boats bring in a variety of fish and shellfish.

10 KEY INDUSTRIES

Agriculture

Fishing

Health Services

1. Agriculture

As the smallest state Rhode Island does not have the vast farmlands of other states, but it still produces a lot of sweet corn, dairy products, and honey.

2. Educational Services

There are 25,550 teachers, administrators, and support workers who help to educate the people of Rhode Island. These represent the whole range from kindergarten teachers to university professors and account for nearly one job in sixteen in the state.

3. Financial Services

There are several large banking and insurance companies in the state, with Providence serving as a financial center in New England. There are 25,850 people who work in these jobs (6.48 percent of the job total).

4. Fishing

With all of that coastline, it's not surprising the state is a center for fishing. The ocean waters provide a variety of fish, mollusks and shellfish, with the lobster gaining prominence among these.

5. Health Services

The biggest employers in the whole state are health care related, with 83,998 jobs in this sector (21.05 percent of all jobs). Doctors, nurses, health-care aides, and those working in retirement homes all count in this category.

RHODE ISLAND

Jewelry

Tourism

Toy Making

6. Jewelry

The state has the highest concentration of jewelry makers in the country, with a reported one thousand jewelry-related companies in operation as of 2013. These include makers of costume jewelry and custom pieces such as engagement rings.

7. Manufacturing

This is the third largest component of the state's economy. The leading products are electrical equipment, which includes light bulb fixtures and surge protectors, and ocean technologies.

8. Marine trades

Nearly 10 percent of the private employers in the state are involved in boating, and it is one area of the economy that is growing. Boat designers, sail makers, marina operators, and marine publishers are just a few of the businesses in this field.

9. Tourism

With access to beaches and historic cities and towns, the state provides a lot of opportunity for vacationers. Primary among the attractions is beautiful Newport. Hotels and restaurants employ more than forty thousand people, making it the second largest industry in the state.

10. Toy Making

Hasbro is one of the top companies to work for in the United States and it is headquartered in Providence. Among its popular games is Monopoly, and the company also makes Transformers and My Little Pony merchandise.

Recipe for Cranberry Muffins

One of three native fruits grown today in large amounts, cranberries were used by Native Americans for food, dyes, and medicine. They introduced European settlers to the fruit, who used it in their cooking—including in delicious muffins such as these.

What You Need

1 ½ cups (355 grams) flour

3 teaspoons (15 milliliters) baking powder

¼ cup (59 g) white sugar

¼ teaspoon (1.2 mL) salt

¼ cup (59 mL) vegetable oil

1 egg beaten

1 cup (237 mL) orange juice

1 tablespoon (15 mL) orange zest

1 ½ cups (355 mL) chopped cranberries

What to Do

•   Preheat oven to 400°F (200°C). Place paper liners in your muffin pan or grease and flour it.

•   Sift flour, salt and baking powder together and set aside.

•   Beat oil and sugar together until they are light. Add the egg and beat until smooth. Add the orange juice and grated zest.

•   Add flour mixture and stir just until mixed. Fold in cranberries.

•   Fill prepared muffin pans two-thirds full and bake for 20 to 25 minutes. Then serve something that could have come from a colonial kitchen.

The Providence Arcade, built in 1828 and the country's first indoor shopping center, was refurbished and reopened in 2013 with shops on the first floor and apartments on the upper levels.

Service Industries

To make up for the decline of manufacturing and to help improve Rhode Island's economy, state officials began, in the 1970s, to try to attract service industries to the region. Today, most of Rhode Island's economy is made up of service jobs, particularly in health care and education. About 26 percent of the state's workforce is employed in health care or education. The state hopes to make itself a center of these growing fields, which it has dubbed "meds and eds."

Health services, the state's largest industry, include doctors' offices, hospitals, and walk-in clinics. In 2011, Brown University opened a new medical school (the only one in the state) about one mile (1.6 km) from its main campus in Providence.

Those who perform educational services, such as teachers and school administrators, also make up a sizable portion of the service industry, as do people who work in finance, insurance, and real estate. Cities such as Providence and Warwick host the headquarters for a number of large banks and other financial institutions.

Tourism

Tourism is a major contributor to the state's economy. It is also the state's fastest-growing industry. The coastal town of Newport draws people from around the world. Its grand

A stroll on the Cliff Walk is a great way to see Newport's Mansions.

mansions are among its most popular destinations. One mansion, Rosecliff, completed in 1902, was modeled after Versailles, the palace of kings in France. Newport's Cliff Walk offers stunning ocean views. In the heart of Newport is the Brick Market Place, filled with shops and restaurants. Nearby is St. Mary's, the oldest Roman Catholic parish in Rhode Island—it was founded in 1828.

Newport also hosts world-famous sporting events. From 1930 to 1983, it was home to the America's Cup yacht races. Every two years in mid-June, the Newport Bermuda Yacht Race is held. Beginning in Newport, boaters race 635 nautical miles (1,175 km) across the ocean to the island of Bermuda. For tennis lovers, the International Tennis Hall of Fame on Newport's historic Bellevue Avenue is open to the public.

During the summer, Newport's annual jazz, folk, and classical musical festivals attract large crowds and talented performers. The jazz and folk festivals take place at Fort Adams in Newport. The classical musical festival is held in Newport's mansions.

There are many recreational firsts in the state that are connected with Newport. The city hosted the first circus performance in what is now the United States in 1774. The first polo match played in the United States was held there is 1876. Five years later, the city was the site for the first U.S. National Lawn Tennis Championship, a tournament that became what we now know as the U.S. Open. The United States Golf Association held the first U.S. Amateur Championship and the first U.S. Open Championship at Newport Golf Club in 1895.

Several nights a year Providence hosts WaterFire. About eighty sparkling bonfires are set ablaze in baskets along three rivers that pass through the middle of the capital city. History lovers are often found on Providence's Benefit Street. Stephen Hopkins's home is located near Benefit Street. Hopkins signed the Declaration of Independence and was Rhode Island's colonial governor from 1755 to 1767.

South of Providence is Warwick—Rhode Island's second-largest city. Warwick is known as the retail capital of Rhode Island. Warwick is also home to Rhode Island's main airport, T.F. Green International Airport.

Farther south, ferries transport people from the fishing village of Galilee to Block Island. The island's quaint inns and serene beaches are not the only draws. Each fall, bird-watchers come to see songbirds that stop on the island on their journey south.

Those wanting to "spin" around Rhode Island can check out the state's many merry-go-rounds. Built in 1876, the Flying Horse Carousel in Westerly may be the oldest in the country. The twenty hand-carved wooden horses are suspended from chains and swing, or "fly out," as the carousel turns.

From its carousels and colonial homes to its developing high-tech, health care, and research industries, Rhode Island has much to offer. The state may have a reputation for being small, but it is certainly big when it comes to possibilities for the future.

A visit to Block Island should include a tour of the Southeast Lighthouse.

RHODE ISLAND
STATE MAP

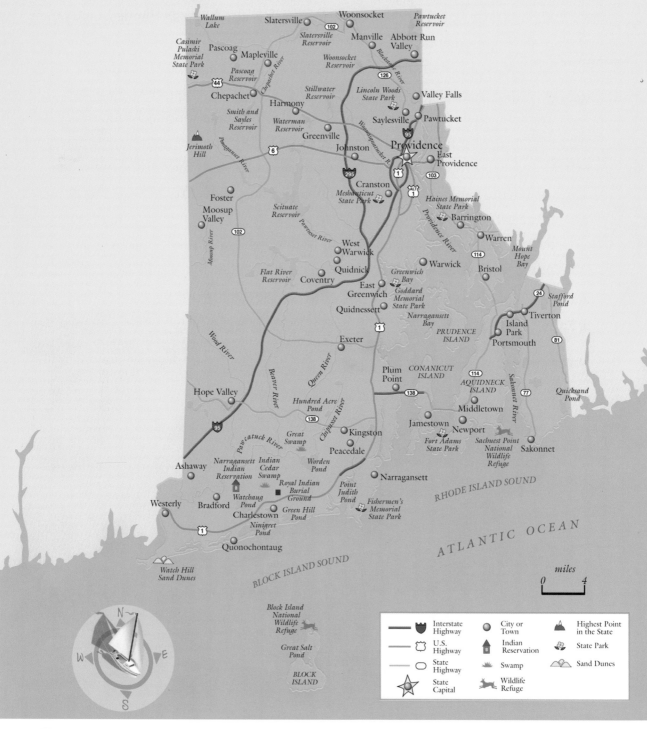

Wallum Lake

Slatersville

Woonsocket

Pawtucket Reservoir

Casimir Pulaski Memorial State Park

Pascoag

Mapleville

102

Slatersville Reservoir

Manville

Abbott Run Valley

Pascoag Reservoir

Chepachet River

Woonsocket Reservoir

126

Blackstone River

44

Chepachet

Stillwater Reservoir

Lincoln Woods State Park

Valley Falls

Harmony

Waterman Reservoir

Saylesville

Pawtucket

Smith and Sayles Reservoir

Greenville

Woonasquatucket R.

95

Jerimoth Hill

Ponaganset River

6

Johnston

Providence

East Providence

1

103

295

ALT 1

Cranston

Haines Memorial State Park

Foster

Meshanticut State Park

Barrington

Providence River

Moosup Valley

Scituate Reservoir

Warren

102

Pawtuxet River

West Warwick

114

Moosup River

Flat River Reservoir

Quidnick

Warwick

Bristol

Mount Hope Bay

Coventry

Greenwich Bay

East Greenwich

Goddard Memorial State Park

24

Stafford Pond

Quidnessett

Narragansett Bay

Island Park

Tiverton

Wood River

Portsmouth

81

Exeter

PRUDENCE ISLAND

Beaver River

Queen River

Plum Point

CONANICUT ISLAND

AQUIDNECK ISLAND

114

Sakonnet River

77

Quicksand Pond

Hope Valley

Hundred Acre Pond

Chipuxet River

138

Middletown

95

138

Kingston

Jamestown

Newport

Pawcatuck River

Great Swamp

Peacedale

Fort Adams State Park

Sachuest Point National Wildlife Refuge

Sakonnet

Ashaway

Narragansett Indian Reservation

Indian Cedar Swamp

Worden Pond

Narragansett

RHODE ISLAND SOUND

Royal Indian Burial Ground

Point Judith Pond

Westerly

Bradford

Watchaug Pond

Green Hill Pond

Fishermen's Memorial State Park

1

Charlestown

Ninigret Pond

ATLANTIC OCEAN

Quonochontaug

Watch Hill Sand Dunes

BLOCK ISLAND SOUND

miles

0   4

Block Island National Wildlife Refuge

Great Salt Pond

BLOCK ISLAND

	Interstate Highway		City or Town		Highest Point in the State
	U.S. Highway		Indian Reservation		State Park
	State Highway		Swamp		Sand Dunes
	State Capital		Wildlife Refuge		

RHODE ISLAND ★ ★ ★
MAP SKILLS

1. Where is the highest point of the state?

2. What large body of water intrudes on the eastern side of Rhode Island?

3. What national wildlife refuges are located on an island?

4. What interstate highway runs north–south along the central part of the state?

5. Jamestown is located on what island?

6. What is the name of the Native American reservation in the southwest part of the state?

7. What U.S. highway would you take to travel from Chepachet to Providence?

8. State Route 114 connects what cities?

9. What water feature is near Abbot Run Valley?

10. Exeter is located near what river?

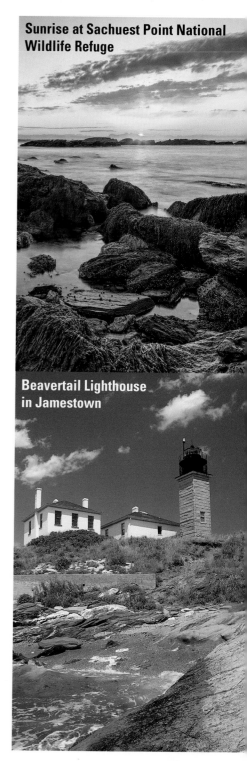

Sunrise at Sachuest Point National Wildlife Refuge

Beavertail Lighthouse in Jamestown

1. Jerimoth Hill
2. Narragansett Bay
3. Sachuest and Block Island National Wildlife Refuges
4. Interstate Highway 95/295
5. Conanicut Island
6. Narragansett Indian Reservation
7. Route 44
8. Middletown, Bristol, Warren, and Barrington
9. Pawtucket Reservoir
10. Queen River

State Flag, Seal, and Song

Rhode Island's state flag features a golden anchor on a white background. Thirteen golden stars, encircling the anchor, represent the original thirteen colonies. Underneath the anchor is a blue ribbon with the word "Hope" in gold. This version of the flag was adopted in 1897.

The state seal depicts a golden anchor with the word "Hope" above it. Written along the circular border of the seal are the words "Seal of the State of Rhode Island and Providence Plantations 1636." Here "1636" represents the year Roger Williams first established Rhode Island's first permanent European settlement. The seal was adopted in 1664.

The official state song is "Rhode Island It's for Me" by Charlie Hall and Maria Day. It was adopted in 1996, replacing "Rhode Island," by T. Clarke Browne. That song was renamed the official state march. For the lyrics, visit:

www.statesymbolsusa.org/Rhode_Island/Song_RhodeIsland.html

Glossary

climate   The average weather conditions of a particular place or region over a period of years.

coastline   All of the land near a shore, especially along the ocean.

commercial   Of, or relating to, business or trade.

economy   The way a system of production, trade, and ownership is arranged.

glacier   A large body of ice moving slowly down a slope or valley or spreading outward on a land surface.

immigrant   A person who comes to a country to live there.

Industrial Revolution   The time of transition to new manufacturing processes from about 1760 to 1840.

industry   The businesses that provide a particular product, service, or manufacturing activity.

longhouse   A long dwelling for several families.

mansion   A large, imposing residence with many rooms.

manufacturing   To make into a product suitable for use from raw materials by hand or by machinery.

Native American   Peoples who lived on the North American continent before the arrival of Europeans.

population   The whole number of people living in a country or region.

reservation   An area of lands reserved especially for use by Native Americans to continue to live by tribal laws and rights.

settler   A person who settles in a new region.

tourism   The practice of traveling for pleasure or the business of encouraging and serving such traveling.

More About Rhode Island

BOOKS

Dell, Pamela. *The Wampanoag*. First Americans. Tarrytown, NY: Marshall Cavendish Benchmark, 2009.

Geake, Robert A. *A History of the Narragansett of Rhode Island: Keepers of the Bay*. Charleston, SC: The History Press, 2011.

Moss, Marissa. *The Bravest Woman in America*. New York, NY: Random House, 2011.

Slavicek, Louise Chipley. *Anne Hutchinson*. Leaders of the Colonial Era. New York, NY: Chelsea House, 2011.

WEBSITES

Narragansett Indian Tribe

www.narragansett-tribe.org

Newport Mansions

www.newportmansions.org

Official Site of the State of Rhode Island

www.ri.gov

AUTHOR

Rick Petreycik is a writer whose articles on history, music, film, and business have appeared in *American Legacy*, *Rolling Stone*, and *Disney* magazines, among other publications.

Lisa M. Herrington is a former executive managing editor at *Weekly Reader*. Growing up, she spent many summer vacations with her family visiting Rhode Island.

Hex Kleinmartin, PhD has taught anthropology, archaeology, and history, and has written several books and papers on these subjects.

Index

Page numbers in **boldface** are illustrations.

Index